About This Book

Title: *Buses*

Step: 1

Word Count: 86

Skills in Focus: All short vowels

Tricky Words: seat, school, more, need, fast, by, now, go

Ideas for Using This Book

Before Reading:

- **Comprehension:** Look at the title and cover image together. Ask readers what they know about buses. What new things do they think they might learn in this book?
- **Accuracy:** Practice saying the tricky words listed on page 1.
- **Phonemic Awareness:** Tell readers you will practice taking apart and putting together the sounds in the word *bus*. Ask readers to tap each finger to their thumb to count the sounds they hear. Ask: How many sounds are in the word *bus*? What is the first sound? Middle sound? End sound? Repeat with other words with short vowel sounds found in the text. Suggested words: *kid*, *sit*, *gas*, *lot*

During Reading:

- Have readers point under each word as they read it.
- **Decoding:** If readers are stuck on a word, help them say each sound and blend the sounds together smoothly. Be sure to point out any short vowel sounds as they appear.
- **Comprehension:** Invite students to talk about what new things they are learning about buses while reading. What are they learning that they didn't know before?

After Reading:

Discuss the book. Some ideas for questions:

- Have you ever ridden on a bus? Describe what it was like.
- What did you learn from the book about why buses are important?

Buses

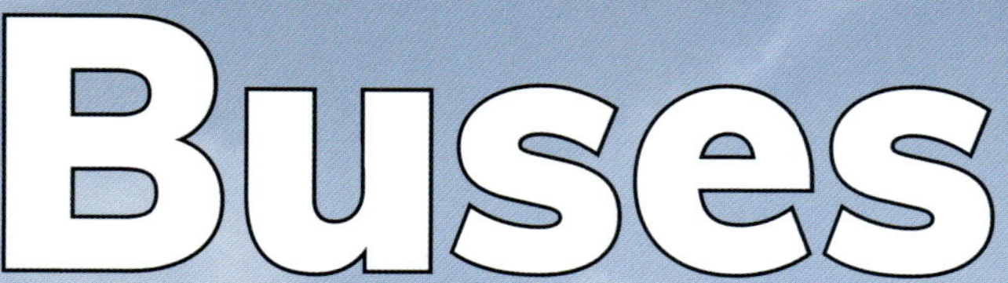

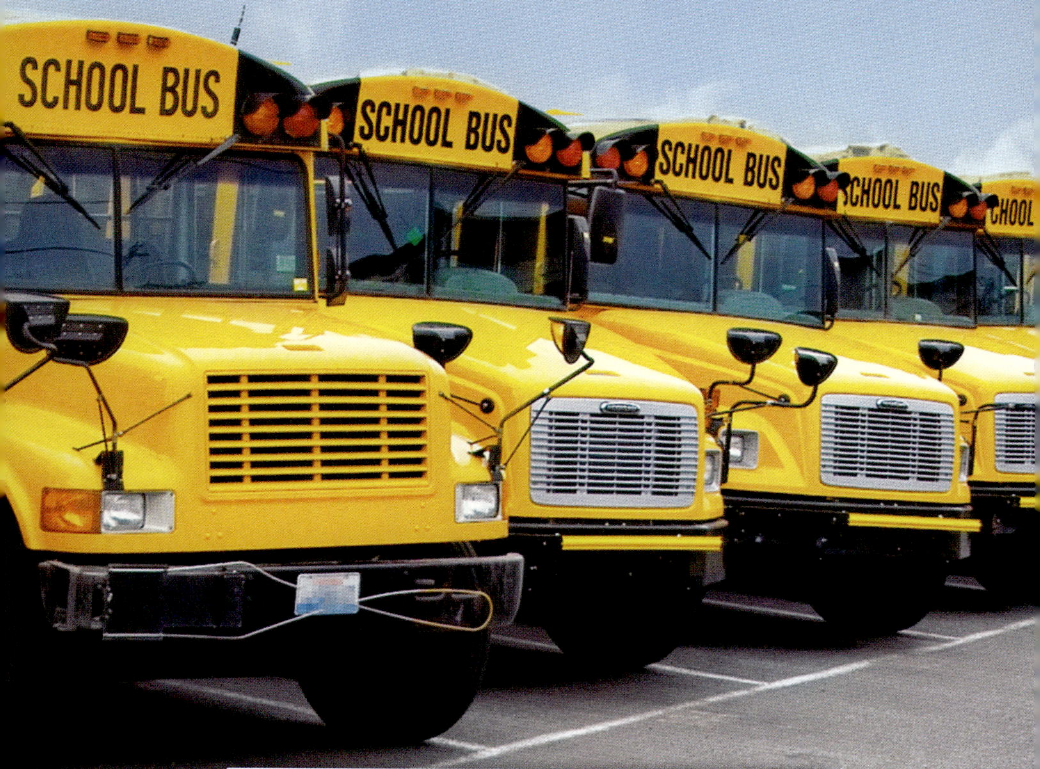

Text by Haley Williams

Reading Consultant
Deborah MacPhee, PhD
Professor, School of Teaching and Learning
Illinois State University

PICTURE WINDOW BOOKS
a capstone imprint

Buses pick up lots of kids.

SCHOOL BUS
300

Buses stop to let kids on.

Kids hop on.

The bus is big.

It has lots of seats.

Kids pick a seat.

Kids sit on the bus.

Liz sits by Ben.

Max sits by Kit.

The bus has to go!

Pat hits the gas.

Buses go fast.

Buses huff and puff.

Buses get kids to school.

Kids get off the bus.

Buses need gas to run.

Pat puts gas in the bus.

Now the bus can
pick up more kids!

More Ideas:

Phonemic Awareness Activity

Practicing Short Vowels:

Tell readers to listen as you stretch out the sounds of a short vowel word. Starting at your left shoulder, tap your right hand down your arm from your shoulder to elbow to wrist as you say each sound slowly. The students will call out the word. Repeat and have students say the sounds with you, moving their right hands down their left arms as they say the sounds. Blend the sounds together smoothly to make the word. Have readers slide their hands smoothly down their arms as they blend the word. Then have readers finger trace the short vowel letter in the air.

Suggested words:

- bus
- sit
- big
- gas
- run

Extended Learning Activity

Play Pretend:

Ask readers to pretend they are riding around on a bus. Where are they sitting on the bus? What kinds of things do they see out the window? Where are they going? Ask readers to share three sentences about riding on the bus. Challenge students to use words with short vowel sounds in their sentences.

Published by Picture Window Books, an imprint of Capstone
1710 Roe Crest Drive, North Mankato, Minnesota 56003
capstonepub.com

Library of Congress Cataloging-in-Publication Data is available on the Library of Congress website.

ISBN: 9798875277061 (hardback)
ISBN: 9798875277023 (paperback)
ISBN: 9798875277009 (eBook PDF)

Image Credits: Getty: FG Trade Latin, 10–11, Fly View Productions, 12, 13, 24, jhorrocks, 2–3, kali9, 4–5, 15, back cover; Shutterstock: Dogora Sun, 18, EdwinPNursalim, 22–23, Inside Creative House, 7, LightField Studios, 14, Michael Vi, 20–21, Pat Shrader, 8–9, Pierre Jean Durieu, 1, 16–17, Prostock-studio, 6, 19, Ronald Sumners, front cover

Printed and bound in China. PO 6460